THE SNIPER

A UNIQUE GLIMPSE AT A SPECIAL OPERATION OF PRAYER

By Deborah B. Vogelzang

Unless otherwise indicated, all scripture quotations are from the New King James Version of the Bible. Scripture quoted from the New King James Version* - Copyright © 1982 by Thomas Nelson. Used by permission. All rights reserved.

Scriptures marked (KJV) are quoted from the King James Version of the Bible in public domain.

THE SNIPER: A UNIQUE GLIMPSE AT A
SPECIAL OPERATION OF PRAYER
ISBN # 978-1-63877-575-1
Copyright © 2021
All rights reserved

Published by Adoration Press
PO Box 1966
Branson, Missouri 65615

Printed in the United States of America. No portion of this book may be reproduced, stored in a retrieval system, or transmitted in any form by any means – electronic, mechanical, photocopy, recording, scanning, or other – except for brief quotations in critical reviews or articles, without prior written permission of the publisher.

CONTENTS

Contents 3
Dedication 5
Preface 7
Introduction 11
    The Battle-Ax 13
The Unfolding 15
    The First Deployment 16
    A Convergence 22
    Rhetoric 26
    For the Last Time 30
Treasure in a Hole 37
BREXIT 43
    Breaking Nations in Pieces 44
    Operation Ophelia Crown 50
    God Will Have His Way 55
The Bigger Threat 59
    A Three-Hour Trance 59
    The Donkey 65
The Shot Heard 'Round the World 69

Setting Things in Order 77
   Submission & Accountability 77
The Testimony of Witnesses 81
   The Prophet 81
   The Apostle 85
   The Teacher 91
   The Donkey 92
   The Apostolic Pastor 94
   The Other Apostle 97
   The Other Sniper 98
   The Other Over-Watch 100
   Closing Thoughts 102
Resources 107
About the Author 111
   Deborah B. Vogelzang 113

DEDICATION

To the over-watch
(My husband and life-long partner),
To all of our wild and brave friends of prayer,
To those who are not afraid enter into realms unseen:

Life truly is a grand adventure!

Enjoy the journey!

PREFACE

In sharing with a friend about the intent of this book, he asked: *"Why write about the sniper?"* For me, the answer was simple.

We are coming into the last of the last days. My husband and I have had decades to learn and develop. We understand the Bible as well as the assignments the Lord has set before us. Yet, for the sake of time, I perceive in my heart that the next generation may not have the luxury of a lifetime to learn. If we can take what has been gleaned from years of study and experience to impart to young lions, we are happy to put it onto the printed page.

Before we offer this opportunity, however, there are a few things we want to make clear. There is no such thing as *the office of the sniper.* It is not a ministerial gift. It is not even a title to be used. Even in the natural realm, snipers are very seldom known by their profession or recognized for the work they do. It is a top-secret, thankless job with little or no public recognition – powerful, yes; public, no.

Do I stand in a ministerial office? Yes, I do. But, that is all we are going to say about it at this time.

Even though I do stand in a five-fold ministry gift, the work of the sniper does not necessarily fall under what might be considered a credentialed ministerial position.

We believe the safest way to view the topic at hand is as *a simple means of illustration*. The Lord has amazing ways to present spiritual truths by painting word pictures or expressing Himself with natural points of illustration.

I would also like to say that the key to being successful with any prayer assignment is for believers to know and understand who they are in Christ. To be effective in the realm of the Spirit, especially against the powers of darkness, believers must have a firm understanding of the Word of God. They must also embrace the authority bestowed in Christ. That is really the secret to success.

Once a believer understands authority, it is still important to develop a broader discipline of knowing the flow of the Spirit – when and how to move in that realm. After grasping the power of Jesus' name, young believers tend to charge headlong into situations – looking to bust some devilhead. When all the while, there is wisdom in approaching a matter with caution and precision.

Preface

Many times, we can side-step actual confrontations with powers of darkness, simply by taking our seat of authority. We are supposed to be enforcers of the victory Jesus has already provided. The actual numbers of real encounters we have had with powers of darkness are few and far between. Mostly, they will be found under our feet. We know who we are and from where the power of our authority lies: seated in Him at the right hand of the Father above.

When it comes to praying for nations, unless an individual believer has a direct connection with a certain country (by birth, citizenship or residence), it is best to wait for direction from the Holy Spirit. He has strategies. God can grant authority. Charging into battle without a plan from above could end up unproductive or worse.

> **2 Corinthians 5:9** – *Therefore we make it our aim… to be well pleasing to Him.*

> **1 Corinthians 2:6** – *However, we speak wisdom among those who are mature, yet not the wisdom of this age, nor of the rulers of this age, who are coming to nothing.*

> **Acts 20:27** – *For I have not shunned to declare to you the whole counsel of God.*

1 Timothy 4:6, 12, 14-16 – *[6]If you instruct the brethren in these things, you will be a good minister of Jesus Christ, nourished in the words of faith and of the good doctrine which you have carefully followed. ... [12]Let no one despise your youth, but be an example to the believers in word, in conduct, in love, in spirit, in faith, in purity. ... [14]Do not neglect the gift that is in you ... [15]Meditate on these things; give yourself entirely to them, that your progress may be evident to all. [16]Take heed to yourself and to the doctrine. Continue in them, for in doing this you will save both yourself and those who hear you.*

2 Timothy 2:15 – *Be diligent to present yourself approved to God, a worker who does not need to be ashamed, rightly dividing the word of truth.*

2 Peter 1:10 – *Therefore, brethren, be even more diligent to make your call and election sure, for if you do these things you will never stumble;* No turning back, no doubting.

INTRODUCTION

Not long before it became popular to equate the work of prayer with military special-operations, there was a word from the Lord that came to me, personal and direct. It was a word I hid in my heart for a few years because it took a while to process.

I love how the Holy Spirit takes time to teach us concerning our own unique giftings. The Lord simply said to me, *"You are a sniper,"* and then began the long process of opening the eyes of my understanding (Ephesians 1:18). It took a while for Him to show me how He had used me in this way – various prayer assignments regarding specific nations over a number of years.

Consider the sniper: a highly skilled soldier with many years of discipline and training. He is an expert marksman. In times of war, he would be the one we want watching our backs. In times of peace, sniper deployments are few, usually considered highly classified missions. When this super-skilled warrior is not actively deployed, he might be found training the troops.

In instances of service or deployment, the sniper is commonly assigned a companion known as the *over-watch* – [handwritten: SWAT Street Walkers!] one who stands by while the sniper focuses upon the target. He has the tools to measure distance, wind speed and direction. He often serves as a communications link and is vigilant in detecting immediate threats.

From the moment my husband heard of what the Lord had decreed over his wife, he knew he was the over-watch. It gave long-awaited definition to a life well-devoted. Moreover, he is very good at his job, both in the natural and in the realm of the Spirit.

As we prepare to examine some of the assignments the Lord has given us concerning the nations, it is important to understand the call. Much of what we do involves prayer, whether working with groups in our own country or taking teams to various destinations abroad.

> ***Jeremiah 1:10*** *– See, I have this day set you over the nations and over the kingdoms, to root out and to pull down, to destroy and to throw down, to build and to plant.*

We know who we are and are not afraid to stand in the place the Lord has prepared for us.

The Battle-Ax

The nickname *Battle-Ax* came through a prophetic word delivered by a highly respected apostle in his land. Standing in a tent meeting in Northern Ireland in June of 2017, he spoke the words of Jeremiah 51:20 nearly word-for-word. At the time, he did not even realize he was quoting a specific text. The experience initially left me crumpled on the floor under the power of God. When he spoke, it came in the first person, as if God Himself were speaking to me:

> *You are My battle-ax and weapon of war: For with you I will break the nations in pieces; With you I will destroy kingdoms.*

The next day began what I will call *the unfolding*.

> **Ephesians 1:18** – *the eyes of your understanding being enlightened; that you may know what is the hope of His calling, what are the riches of the glory of His inheritance in the saints,*

THE UNFOLDING

It started with a question from the Lord, *"Where did World War I start?"* In that moment, I had no idea the answer. It had been too many years since we had studied it in school.

Finding ourselves with limited research tools in our hotel room, a quick search of the internet revealed the first shots of the Great War were fired in Sarajevo, Yugoslavia on 28 June 1914.[1] Even though Yugoslavia technically no longer exists[2] (currently divided into several nations), I recognized immediately why the Lord might ask me such a question. Yet, I had no idea that He was about to pull back the curtain and reveal a connection between multiple prayer assignments that spanned more than three decades. There was a common thread which I had never noticed.

From as far back as primary school, a couple of Eastern European countries were foremost in my heart. They were nearly neighbors – Czechoslovakia[3] (now divided into two nations) and Yugoslavia. If given a geography assignment in class, these were the nations I would select. I had done much research and written many reports, even from a young age. In my youth, they were Cold War era communist countries in what was then known as the *Eastern Bloc*.[4]

As a young adult attending Bible school far from home, these two nations came up once again. As it was from my youth, my heart still yearned to see them free.

The First Deployment

In the spring of 1987, I and a friend attended a special service where those in attendance were instructed to prophesy to the nations. The speaker, a wonderful Bible teacher, indicated that the Holy Spirit would *quicken* in our hearts a nation and then we were to prophesy. I had never dreamed of doing such a thing. At first I did not understand, yet up it came from my heart: *Czechoslovakia*. I do not remember what I said, but I did my best to utter whatever I felt inspired to say in the moment. I certainly wish now that I had written it down.

The teacher went on to explain that we should expect whatever nation the Lord had attached to our prophesying to be seen in the news within the next three days. Much to my surprise, while flipping through television channels a couple days later, I caught a report about a certain communist leader. For some reason he had been forced to cancel his trip to Czechoslovakia.[5] I could hardly believe my ears.

Much later that same night, I found myself praying in the Spirit in other tongues. In many respects, I was experimenting with this new found opportunity to prophesy over nations. I did *not* know what I was doing, but I was certainly willing to make myself available to the Lord. Before I knew what was happening, in the Spirit, my living room floor became overlaid with what seemed like a map of Yugoslavia. The moments that followed are forever imprinted upon my mind.

I could see various regions of that country bound by different types of demonic activity. Perhaps the areas were what is now become many different nations. At any rate, I could see a stronghold of cancer over here; another sort of illness over there; poverty was everywhere... As each adversarial concentration was revealed, as the Word of God teaches, I would simply bind and/or loose in the name of Jesus (Matthew 18:18). It was thrilling to work with the Lord in this way. Yet, what transpired next caught me by surprise.

Ephesians 6:12-13 – *For we do not wrestle against flesh and blood, but against principalities, against powers, against the rulers of the darkness of this age, against spiritual hosts of wickedness in the heavenly places. Therefore take up the whole armor of God, that you may be able to withstand in the evil day, and having done all, to stand.*

Before I knew what happened, there was a dark figure standing in front of me – literally, right in my face. It was a very large, black-cloud-of-a-thing that towered over me. In a menacing tone, I heard him say, *"What are you doing here? What do you think you're doing?"* It was a much darker force than the lower level principalities or powers I had addressed previously. Perhaps it was a ruler of darkness or maybe a spiritual *host* of wickedness? He did kind of come to greet me.

What was I to do? I did not have an answer for his questions. I had simply been following the Holy Ghost, or so I thought. Clearly, I did not know what I was doing. Yet, there was something very big and powerful that rose up out of my innermost being. I think we might call it a *roar*?

I stepped back on my right heel, as if to brace myself. I pointed my right index finger in the direction from which the voice came and said, *"You! You have to go, in Jesus' Name!"* There was no fear. Yet, there was a power which I had not yet known proceeding out of my mouth.

Note to self: Apparently, it is not important to have an answer for questions posed by powers of darkness when one is possessed by the Greater One on the inside (1 John 4:4). We are to *open our mouths wide, and He will fill it* (Psalm 81:10)!

Instantaneously, he departed. I felt the force of the speed in which he fled. As quickly as he could move, he was gone – faster than a speeding bullet. There was a sound to it, which is impossible to convey on the printed page. *Phwing!* He was out of sight, never to return.

I finished working with the Holy Spirit in prayer over that nation and then off to bed I went. I slept like a baby, without fear or concern. Little did I know I had just completed my first *sniper* assignment?

Disclaimer: I now fully understand that this was not a model assignment. In many respects, I was simply *messing around* in prayer, without any specific direction or intent. There were no orders for deployment.

The Sniper: A Unique Glimpse at a Special Operation of Prayer

The reader should also note that in every other sniper assignment about which we will share: there is an over-watch, prayer group or team in the equation. Remember, snipers do not work alone. Jesus sent the disciples out two by two for good reason (Matthew 11:2; 21:1, Mark 11:1, Luke 10:1; 19:29). Snipers are viewed as solitary, yet they almost always have someone standing by. *SWAT – Recruits for Sniper Status!*

SWAT
Street
Walkers

Also to be noted, powers of darkness have a certain right to operate in the affairs of nations. It has to do with Adam's sin. (This subject alone could be a topic for another entire book.) When Jesus returns to set His feet on the Mount of Olives, their evil reign will come to its final end. In the meantime, believers must be watchful not to overstep our bounds, operating within the authority of Christ under His blood and in His name.

Demonic strongholds are only part of the equation. Too often, believers want to deal with powers of darkness in the heavenlies (Ephesians 6:12), yet fail to address strongholds in the minds of people (2 Corinthians 10:3-5). We can bind the devil all day long, but if the minds of the people are not renewed and patterns of thinking or behavior changed (Romans 12:1-2), then victory

SWAT wt. Recruit for those wanting Rom 12:2

will be short-lived, at best. Deliverance begins at the foot of the cross.

At the time, did I know who I was in Christ? Yes, in a measure, perhaps I knew. Did I learn from the experience? Yes, absolutely, though I did not consider or speak of it for many years. Was something gained? God has ways of turning our ignorance and mistakes into powerful testimonies. The ground taken in that moment would prove to be a success that has followed me throughout the decades, though I did not know of it for more than 30 years.

Once we learn to operate from the seated position of authority in Christ, brush-ups with powers of darkness should be rare. When or IF we have such encounters, it is the blood of Jesus that marks us *safe* and protected from such volatile adversaries. Knowing and hearing and speaking as He leads + controls my

2 Corinthians 2:14 – Now thanks be to God vocals who always leads us in triumph in Christ, and through us diffuses the fragrance of His knowledge in every place.

Matthew 18:18 – Assuredly, I say to you, whatever you bind on earth will be bound in heaven, and whatever you loose on earth will be loosed in heaven.

1 John 4:4 – *You are of God, little children, and have overcome them, because He who is in you is greater than he who is in the world.*

Psalm 81:10 – *...Open your mouth wide, and I will fill it.*

2 Corinthians 10:3-5 – *For though we walk in the flesh, we do not war according to the flesh. For the weapons of our warfare are not carnal but mighty in God for pulling down strongholds, casting down arguments and every high thing that exalts itself against the knowledge of God, bringing every thought into captivity to the obedience of Christ,*

Romans 12:1-2 – *I beseech you therefore, brethren, by the mercies of God, that you present your bodies a living sacrifice, holy, acceptable to God, which is your reasonable service. And do not be conformed to this world, but be transformed by the renewing of your mind, that you may prove what is that good and acceptable and perfect will of God.*

A Convergence

I will take a moment here to give a little history lesson and tell of a vision I had in the fall of 1997. It is relevant to the unfolding.

The Berlin Wall fell in 1989, marking the end of the Cold War and the beginning of the end of communism in Eastern Europe.[6]

How is it that the Berlin wall fell? The simple answer would be prayer. Much prayer was made over many decades by thousands of people. Real change began to manifest as believers behind the Iron Curtain took hold of their authority in Christ (Ephesians 1:17-23; 2:6), reigning over communism on the basis of the blood in the name of Jesus.

My entire childhood was spent watching the Cold War play out in the news. When the wall fell, it was like watching a very surreal dream.

> ***Psalm 126:1-3*** *– When the LORD brought back the captivity of Zion, We were like those who dream. Then our mouth was filled with laughter, And our tongue with singing. Then they said among the nations, "The LORD has done great things for them." The LORD has done great things for us, and we are glad.*

Seemingly, one minute there was communism in Eastern Europe and the next minute it was over – long after a lifetime of heartache for millions. Czechoslovakia peacefully separated into two nations at the beginning of 1993.[7] Yugoslavia subsequently broke into several nations over a series of political conflicts during the early 1990s.[8]

Let us take a moment to remind ourselves that World War I started in Sarajevo, Yugoslavia. There was much oppression and demonic activity in the area over many decades (perhaps centuries), with this region at the center of it.

Right around the same time that Yugoslavia and Czechoslovakia split into several nations, North Korea began a long season of famine. Historically, it became known as the March of Suffering – a period of economic crisis and starvation (1994 to 1998). Approximately 15% of the population eventually died as a result.[9]

While much of the above historical moments were happening, as a busy wife and young mother, I personally knew very little of it. Yet, by the fall of 1997, the peak of North Korea's plight was being reported widely through international news outlets. Almost daily, I would hear myself saying to the Lord, *"Someone needs to be praying about North Korea."*

During a prayer conference in October of 1997, the conference host called for a special session. North Korea was in dire need of prayer. I made it a point to be there, along with several hundred others. Much to my surprise, as I stood at my seat making my supply in the Spirit, I had an open vision:

> *I saw a map of Europe and Asia. It seemed like an historic movie of something that happened right around the same time as the fall of the Iron Curtain. I saw a large group of demonic spirits leave Eastern Europe and converge in the one place in the world where they would still be welcome. They converged on North Korea.*

I remember wondering why the Lord would show me such a thing. At the time, from my seat in the auditorium, I prayed as best I could. Yet, until more was revealed I would hide it in my heart for another day. I figured if the Lord had more for me to do with it, He would let me know.

After careful study of the timeline outlined above, it is easy to see that the demonic spirits in the 1997 vision likely came from the neighborhood of the Eastern Bloc countries. It never occurred to me in 1997 that the spirits I saw in the vision were likely some of the same ones I had dealt with from my living room in 1987.

Ephesians 1:17-23; 2:6 – 17 *that the God of our Lord Jesus Christ, the Father of glory, may give to you the spirit of wisdom and revelation in the knowledge of Him, 18 the eyes of your understanding being enlightened; that you may know what is the hope of His calling, what are the riches of the glory of His inheritance in the saints, 19 and what is the exceeding greatness of His power toward us who believe, according to the working of His mighty power 20 which He worked in Christ when He raised Him from the dead and seated Him at His right hand in the heavenly places, 21 far above all principality and power and might and dominion, and every name that is named, not only in this age but also in that which is to come. 22 And He put all things under His feet, and gave Him to be head over all things to the church, 23 which is His body, the fullness of Him who fills all in all…6 and raised us up together, and made us sit together in the heavenly places in Christ Jesus*

Rhetoric

As the unfolding continued, the Lord took me back to the summer of 2013. By this time, North Korea was regularly breathing out rhetoric against the United States, threatening nuclear attack. Day-after-day it was reported in the news. And every time I saw or heard of it, I would say, *"Lord, someone needs to be praying about North Korea."*

When it comes to praying for nations, it is important to use restraint and good judgment before tearing headlong into a battle. It is better to take time to prepare. I waited. I held it before the Father, asking Him to have people pray. Yet, I did not pray about it myself. I waited and watched while others prayed. For what was I waiting? I was waiting for direction. I was waiting to be deployed, though that term was not familiar to me at the time.

Then one day in June, the word of the Lord came unto me saying, *"I want you to pray about North Korea."* I thought, *"You do?"* and then wondered what I could possibly do about it. Then He brought to my remembrance the vision I had had *15 years* before regarding this same despotic nation. He let me see what I would be dealing with. The vision had been sitting on the shelf for well more than a decade. Now He was suddenly bringing it back to my remembrance. Wow!

He then said, *"You know what to do."* I thought, *"I do."*

Once I knew what we were dealing with, the assignment seemed simple enough. Demonic spirits subject to the name of Jesus: How hard could that be?

I picked up the telephone and called my prayer partner. I said, *"The Lord wants us to pray about North Korea."* She said, *"Okay. I'll meet you at the church at lunch."*

On this particular day, my prayer partner took on the role of over-watch. Though in those days, neither of us knew anything about such a job description.

We worshipped, following the Holy Spirit as we moved into the realms of glory. Then the unction came. It was an anointing greater than either of us had ever known in prayer.

We were dealing with low level principalities and powers attempting to escalate to war. Rhetoric; we were dealing with nothing more than rhetoric. Those spirits needed to be put under a gag order. We did what the Holy Spirit inspired us to do and proclaimed what He told us to declare.

I will say there was an extremely powerful anointing from the Holy Ghost that day. I am certain they heard us all the way to North Korea.

The Unfolding

It was a powerful unction. We opened our mouths and a raging river *roared*.

In the realm of the spirit, we put those demons in a box with a lid and sealed them inside under the Blood. We put them on *mute* and commanded them to cease with their antics.

Seemingly overnight, the constant barrage in the media ceased; the deluge of empty threats subsided. That one prayer session (added to many others, I am sure) brought for the United States nearly two years of reprieve. It was a turning point.

Of course there had been hundreds, if not thousands, of people praying about the situation. Yet it took some time for their prayers to build up a place in the Spirit from which a shot could be taken. We (my prayer partner and I) simply climbed up on the backs of all those other prayers, took aim and fired. It took us a total of 15 minutes, start to finish.

As a point of illustration, when a sniper is deployed over a great distance, regardless of his own branch of the military, other branches of service may be involved in his deployment. For example, as an Army ranger, he may ride in an Air Force jet, sail on a Naval vessel or be escorted in country by the Marines. I realize that may not really be the case, but for the sake of illustration, the point has been made.

As it goes with the sniper, so it goes with prayer. It sometimes takes the prayers of many saints, many groups over an extended period of time to establish a place from which the sniper is able to do his or her job. Once the way is prepared, it is easy enough for the sniper to be deployed, climbing up inside the prayers of others to take the shot.

For the Last Time

In April of 2017, while preparing to take a prayer team on a journey, the Lord spoke to my heart and said, *"While you are in Ireland, you will be praying about North Korea."* By this time, their nuclear threats were no longer empty. They had acquired the technology and were actively engaged in escalation toward war. Our new President had his hands full. The threat of World War III loomed.

I remember thinking, *"North Korea? Really?"* I thought it odd to carry such an assignment all the way to Europe. So I put the admonition on the shelf and quite frankly forgot about it. There were other assignments to be undertaken.

The purpose of this trip to Ireland was to pray in advance of a nation-wide evangelistic outreach. Hundreds of ministers from across the globe were schedule to converge there in June of that same year. As we landed in Dublin, there were four on team. We covered the whole of the island with many wonderful testimonies to bring home – 1,500 miles in 12 days – *phew*!

The last stop of the journey was Derry/Londonderry, Northern Ireland. For those familiar with Northern Ireland's tumultuous history, Derry/Londonderry is the place where *the troubles* started in 1969.[10] It led to decades of bloody civil war.

We arrived late at night, going straight to our hotel intending to finish our journey into the city the next day. When we put our feet on the floor the next morning, international news reported further escalation by North Korea against the United States. Suddenly, the Lord's instructions rang once again in my ears and instantly I knew what we were to do.

The civil war in Northern Ireland ended around the turn of the century and was commemorated by the building of the Peace Bridge in Derry/Londonderry.[11] After breakfast we hopped into the car and immediately headed for the Peace Bridge to pray. In our haste, we took a wrong turn and ended up at the base of the bridge, perhaps by God's design. Foundations for peace are important, are they not? – Especially when facing the threat of nuclear war.

This assignment was different from those previously described. There seemed to be urgency in the making. There were four of us, which required a little more effort to flow together in unity. As we pressed in, it was amazing to see how it all unfolded.

Once in the realm of the Spirit, we moved into what I will call *stealth* mode. Two stood watch and kept us covered under the blood of Christ; two pressed forward into the realm of the unseen. There was no vision. It seemed as though we were working *in the dark* - like a top secret assignment.

It was almost as if the Lord took us all the way to Ireland so we could work undetected in the unseen realm. We sensed a great relevance to the location: the Peace Bridge. It was a powerful platform from which to pray.

In *stealth* mode, I had a sense there were many others gathered there for the same assignment. I thought, *"Lord, how many are gathered here?"* Immediately, upon thinking that thought, the bells in the church tower across the river rang out 12 times. We were not alone, even in what seemed like the dark.

Twelve is the number for government – God's hand at work in the affairs of men. It seemed as though we were deployed on assignment with an entire crew gathered from various places around the earth, meeting in the realms of glory to take the shot.

It was 12 noon in Northern Ireland; 7 a.m. in Washington D.C. Regarding the situation, the President of the United States had a security briefing with the Senate at 9 a.m. It was from this point forward that he began to take bold steps to defuse the matter. The beating drums for war began to fade into the distance.

As of this writing, the Lord has not asked us to pray again specifically regarding North Korea. Yet, standing in my hotel in Northern Ireland two months later, I wept as the Lord pulled back the curtain to help me see how it was all connected.

In the unfolding, the Lord made me to understand that I had been dealing with the same demonic spirits since 1987 – the same spirits that had been involved with inciting World War I in Sarajevo, Yugoslavia. These are some of the same spirits intent on inciting world war once again.

Having said all this about the sniper, we don't want to take away from the day-to-day operations of prayer. There are many who pray for nations such as North Korea on a daily basis. They pray according to:

> **1 Timothy 2:1-2** *–...for kings and all in the authority, that we may lead a quiet and peaceable life.*

They pray in the Holy Spirit in other tongues. Each day they pray as they are directed to pray, seated in their position of authority in Christ Jesus.

God has an army of believers, each one making his or her supply in the Spirit (Ephesians 4:16, Philippians 1:19). We must never glorify one function over another. Endeavor to understand our own giftings we must, and then do what He says to do with them. This book is being written that we may know it is possible to understand ones giftings and the gifts of others.

Prayer victories are very rarely the success of one individual alone. Just when we think we have prayed something through, the Lord will bring someone across our path that has been praying about the same thing – longer, harder, faster, better.

Let us not be competitive with one another or think of ourselves more highly than we ought to think (Romans 12:3). Instead, let us recognize that every member of the body of Christ has a job to do. We need each other. We are only complete altogether in Him.

In this the last of the last days, believers must know who we are in Christ. We must be about our Father's business.

> ***Philippians 1:19*** *– For I know that this will turn out for my deliverance through your prayer and the supply of the Spirit of Jesus Christ,*
>
> ***Ephesians 4:13-16*** *– ¹³till we all come to the unity of the faith and of the knowledge of the Son of God, to a perfect man, to the measure of the stature of the fullness of Christ; ¹⁴that we should no longer be children, tossed to and fro and carried about with every wind of doctrine, by the trickery of men, in the*

cunning craftiness of deceitful plotting, [15]but, speaking the truth in love, may grow up in all things into Him who is the head--Christ--[16]from whom the whole body, joined and knit together by what every joint supplies, according to the effective working by which every part does its share, causes growth of the body for the edifying of itself in love.

TREASURE IN A HOLE

In military terms, it is important to understand that it is possible for several covert operations to be deployed simultaneously. If we were to journal the contents of this book chronologically, it could be difficult to follow. Therefore, to avoid confusion, we have opted to present the accounts by assignment.

The United States of America went to war in Afghanistan against the Taliban late in 2001.[12] The invasion was in response to the terrorist attacks of 11 September that same year. In the spring of 2003, U.S. troops also found their way into Iraq on an errand to wrap up some unfinished business.[13] Initially, they were successful in the deployment, yet the despotic dictator Saddam Hussein eluded capture for many months.

It was also during 2003 that my husband and I moved our family to a small town in the Midwest to pioneer a local church. We began with weekly prayer meetings and Bible studies in July, launching the church full-time the following January. We found great fulfillment in developing and training disciples.

The Sniper: A Unique Glimpse at a Special Operation of Prayer

The highlight of each week for me was the Thursday noon-time prayer group that met in our home. All the ladies who participated had come into the fullness of the Spirit under our ministry. I had personally laid hands on each one to be filled with the Holy Spirit with the evidence of speaking in other tongues. Their hearts were so pure before God and they were so teachable it was a joy to lead them in prayer every week.

These women sacrificed their lunch-hour to come and pray together. Most weeks, we would pray about various community development projects, but occasionally the Lord would redirect. On 11 December, the ladies all came with one particular thing on their hearts. They wanted to pray for our soldiers.

Reports of war had become common place as efforts in the respective theatres of war dragged on. On this particular day, the ladies had been hearing terrible things in the news and thought our soldiers were in need of additional prayer support.

Unified in the assignment, it was easy to move into the realms of glory. In no time at all, it seemed as if we were standing on a mountainside in Afghanistan speaking words of encouragement to battle-weary soldiers. It was beautiful. The unction came quickly and easily. It was as though we had *prayed through* in a rather short period of time.

Then something strange happened – something out of the ordinary flow of our prayer meetings. It seemed as though there was a shift in the Spirit – like we changed locations – like we took a hard turn to the left? In this place, it was dark – much like *stealth* mode described in the previous chapter.

Personally, I did not know where we were or what we were doing. We were following the Holy Spirit, praying in other tongues. It took some effort to stay in unity and preserve the flow as we moved in the Spirit. Then, I heard myself saying the strangest things, as if I were speaking to a soldier:

Look in that hole!
See that <u>treasure</u> in that hole!
<u>Get</u> – that – <u>treasure</u> – out – of – that - <u>hole</u>!

The Holy Spirit inspired those words to be uttered and they did not come just once, but repeatedly. Over and over they poured out of my mouth; each time with more authority and urgency than the time before.

I will interject here, I *thought* it was probably one of the silliest things I had ever done in prayer. Those words made no sense to the natural mind. It was almost embarrassing to think I was saying such ridiculous phrases in front of all these young believers.

Note 1: When moving in the Spirit in prayer – our heads may be screaming one thing, while our spirits are uttering the very oracles of God.

As quickly as we had moved into *stealth* mode, prayer was over in like manner. The unction had ended and our time together was finished. It was all very strange. When we wrapped up, we were still standing *in the dark* having no clue as to what we had done.

When I opened my eyes and looked around the room, all the ladies were staring at me, questioningly. One said, *"What was that all about?!?"* I said, *"I don't know, but we're not going to talk about it. We're just going to wait and see what happens."* We left the meeting under a Holy Ghost gag order.

Note 2: What happens in the prayer closet is sometimes best left in the prayer closet. Too many times we over think and talk ourselves right out of the victory.

By Sunday afternoon, 14 December, news was breaking that a certain fugitive had been captured in the night near Tikrit, Iraq (a time difference of seven hours). 13 December 2003, Saddam Hussein was found in a hole with a couple of weapons and three-quarters-of-a-million U.S. dollars.[14]

Believers had been praying for months regarding the capture of Saddam Hussein. Up to that point, I had not personally prayed about it. Even in the meeting described above, we did not know the subject of our prayer. We were following the Holy Spirit. We were praying for soldiers. Little did we know we were praying for those who would eventually capture this despicable adversary?

Yet, the Lord had need of a sniper. He needed someone who could climb up in the realm of the Spirit, inside the tower of prayer that had been built by others – someone who, by faith, could take the shot.

On 11 December, it was our turn to be deployed – long before we ever knew such special operations existed in the realms of prayer. It has been said that a certain prophet proclaimed right around that same time that *"Saddam Hussein would be captured in three days."*

Regardless of the timeline, God had His way and we are first-hand witnesses to the power of unified prayer – the function of a special operation that was laid out before us.

We were fully aware that others were praying and that we were not alone in the endeavor. Every prayer counts in the realms of glory.

When the group reassembled on 18 December, we were all speechless – humbled beyond words to think of how to Lord had used us for His purposes.

Solitary though they may be, in the grand scheme of things, even snipers seldom work alone.

> ***2 Corinthians 4:7*** *– But we have this treasure in earthen vessels, that the excellence of the power may be of God and not of us.*

BREXIT

Please allow me to start this segment by saying: Politics can be very complicated, especially in the many nations of Europe. We have learned much through many journeys, but I have never formally studied the subject. Hopefully, we will be able to share enough good information to make the necessary points.

There once was a thing called BREXIT (British Exit). Simply defined, it was the intent of the British people to formally exit the European Union (EU). The United Kingdom (UK – aka Great Britain) determined by popular vote in the summer of 2016 to end their membership in the EU.

The European Union was and still is thought by some to be a prophetic reviving of the ancient Roman Empire. As it stands, it is a collective European government. Poorer nations joined and suddenly the wealth of their neighbors came to their aid. It seemed like a grand experiment that only brought complex problems to wealthier economies within.

We have seen first-hand the beautiful super highways that were built in places previously considered third-world countries. We have also witnessed the devastating results of poor immigration policies as a whole. Many exchanged their own national identities for an ambiguous continental demographic. It is my opinion that the UK was smart to get out while they could.

From the start, it seemed to be a bad deal for the British – in nearly every way one could imagine, but especially economically. Some believe now that the EU may be destined to ultimately collapse as other nations line up to follow the UK's example.

As of this writing, some of the details of BREXIT are *still* hanging in the balance. Yet, in my heart I know that God intends for the UK to depart the EU, even if only for a season.

Politics can be tricky. Timing is everything. The future is yet to be determined.

Breaking Nations in Pieces

The United Kingdom is made up of a coalition of the four distinct identities of Great Britain: England, Northern Ireland, Scotland and Wales. Simplified, each member nation has its own governing Assembly with the Houses of Parliament in London overseeing common interests. In terms of U.S. government, I would liken it to *state* and *federal* oversight. It is one country with many members, not counting those once considered part of the British Commonwealth of Nations.

As stated in a previous chapter, Northern Ireland and Ireland have a tumultuous past. Some of the most despotic terrorists in the world came out of this island. Plagued by long-term civil war, it has been a place of much disagreement – the epitome of division.

Once formal peace agreements were drafted around the turn of the century, the Northern Ireland Assembly was then able to govern its own little corner of the UK. Even though divisions were still evident and peace fragile, they had managed to get along well enough.

Yet, that all came into question one Saturday morning in December of 2016. A group of unassuming men and women were invited to tour an historic government building near Belfast. Northern Ireland's Assembly is housed in Stormont – a beautiful monolith that marks the landscape with great hope and endurance.

On this particular day, as these precious men and women of God converged for a time of prayer, it was not just any gathering. It was a moment in time imprinted upon all of us – a defining moment in history – though most people will never know enough to connect the dots. It was an assignment that none of us could have completed alone. This nation had a date with destiny and there were watchers sent to witness the Hand of God as it swept in.

Invited as guests to tour Stormont, gracious hosts had granted access to the strategy room of the leading political party of the land. It was a nice meeting space with a large conference table. So after roaming through the parliament chambers on the ground floor, the group ascended to the upper level for a time of prayer.

Numbered in the group were no less than a dozen authentic apostles and prophets (guests and hosts, alike). They came together to pray for this divided land. They came to this seat of authority to petition Almighty God for a sovereign move of His Hand. I expect that no one in the room that day would have anticipated the end result of such an entreaty.

This author is certain that each attendee would have their own account to share of the story – from their own particular vantage point. Yet, from this author's perspective, the only part that is fair to share is the side to which I am directly a witness.

Everyone had something to offer in prayer that day. Some petitions were similar while others were unique. When one of the hosts asked me to step forward to pray, the presence of God had already filled the room. Yet, a power descended upon me in an unusual way. Shaking, I rose from my seat.

As I pressed forward, I saw with my own eyes angels descending into the room where we were assembled and heard myself declaring this place to be *Bethel*. (Apparently, though the people of Northern Ireland thought Stormont was theirs, God proclaimed it as *His House* on that day?) One apostle had previously asked for hidden things to be revealed. I do remember echoing that request and then continued to pray with authority in the Spirit as I returned to my seat.

It was all very surreal. I remember thinking, *"What is going on?"*

When I sat down, I wept and wept under the power of God. I learned later that the selected seat just happened to be the chair belonging to the First Minister. She was the leader of her party and consequently, the chief political figure in that realm. All I can say is that I felt much sorrow and pain for her as I sat there weeping in her place.

When prayer was over, a somber mood settled upon us all. We knew we had touched heaven, yet I seriously doubt any of us could have imagined that less than a week later, Northern Ireland's government would completely fall apart.[15]

It failed so miserably that eventually London was forced to govern this troubled land for a period of years. For some, it seemed like a long season, but in due course all those accused of corruption were eventually cleared, including the First Minister who held her ground throughout the tumult.[16]

Three months later (21 March 2017), the opposition leader and deputy First Minister died.[17] At one time, to put it kindly, he had been a violent leader in the IRA (Irish Republican Army). In his later years he yielded to more peaceful means of negotiation. His death complicated the political climate in Northern Ireland even further.

At several points throughout the course of the scandal, some of our friends would ask us periodically to return saying, *"Please come and help us put our government back together."* In reality, it was the Lord Who orchestrated the entire upheaval, and it was the Lord Who would be responsible for the divine timing of the restoration thereof.

Several months after the tour, we did return to Stormont privately – a small group of three. The building was in essence closed for business. As we wandered through the great halls of this grand facility I saw giant angels standing guard. I had the distinct impression that they were there to insure it would remain tightly shut up. I cannot explain how I knew, but in my heart it was clear that Stormont would remain closed until BREXIT was done.[18] Perhaps an angel told me?

Why would it be so important to God for Northern Ireland's Assembly to be scattered? There are many reasons, I suppose. A time for repentance certainly comes to the top of the list. Yet, in my heart I know it had much to do with BREXIT.

Interestingly enough, six months after the collapse of the Assembly in Northern Ireland, the UK held a national election (June of 2017). As a result, the conservative party of Northern Ireland (the DUP – Democratic Unionist Party) had such a sweeping victory they became the second most powerful party in all of Great Britain. They won no less than 10 seats in the House of Commons in London.

Turns out, the DUP are a stubborn lot. God used them powerfully as a unified voice in London throughout the entire BREXIT process. They held the feet of the Prime Minister to the fire and refused to allow any compromise. They were a voice of righteousness at a time when God needed to be heard. Had they not held such a position, it is likely that Britain would have been severely hindered in their ability to exit the EU within the prescribed time.

The House of Commons (aka Britain's Parliament) gave final approval to BREXIT on 9 January 2020.[19] Northern Ireland's Assembly resumed business in Stormont less than one week later.[18] 31 January 2020 marked the end of the United Kingdom's official membership in the European Union.

Only history will show how long that status will remain intact. At this time, there is great value in not being included in what could become one-world government; laying the foundation for the future kingdom of the anti-Christ.

Operation Ophelia Crown

A cursory study of military practice makes it easy to grasp the idea of code names being used for specific operations. For example, the U.S. code name for the capture of Saddam Hussein was *Operation Red Dawn*. *Operation Overlord* was the code name used for the massive undertaking commonly known as D-Day – the allied forces invasion of Normandy in World War II. Most of these types of codes are confidential for an extended period of time and only declassified when it is safe for public consumption.

In scripture we can see that God refers to Himself by different titles depending upon the operation (i.e. the Lord of Hosts [the God of Angel Armies], Elohim, YHWH, etc.). Jesus is also known by many names: Son of Man, King of Kings, Messiah, Savior, etc. These are all in essence identifiers and code names. When we need provision, we call upon El Shaddai – the God is Who is more than enough. When we need a Savior, we call upon Jesus - the Lamb of God Who takes away the sins of the world.

In the fall of 2018, little did we know that God was about to introduce us to a special operation, complete with a code name. At the time, BREXIT was still engaged in major negotiations, both within the UK and without.

We had gone into London to attend a prayer conference. Our hosts encouraged a prayer-walk of the city. On a rare sunny day in October, we eventually found ourselves standing in front of the Palace of Westminster, near the historic statue of King Richard, the Lion Heart. The Palace of Westminster, among other things, includes the House of Lords and the House of Commons.

Standing in front of that statue, suddenly the Holy Spirit arrested me. Upon me He fell so strongly that I dare not move. We stood there a long time watching the Ministers of Parliament (MPs) return from their lunch.

When the sun finally peaked around the south tower, the stones of the buildings lit up in a lovely shade of amber. In that moment, I recognized the scene. Had I been there before in a vision?

From my journal dated 2 January 2012, the following account can be discovered:

> I found myself in a place of government. Approaching a large wooden door, a woman met me there. She escorted me up a beautiful wooden staircase inside the tower. Apparently, I was scheduled to speak. As I waited in the room where she left me to prepare, outside the window I could see many stately buildings – all with a beautiful amber hue.

*When the woman returned, she presented a skirt suit for me to wear during my appointment. With a wink she said, "You are going to need this. It is on loan from **Ophelia Crown**."*

At the time of the vision, I thought the place of government to be a heavenly scene. It did not occur to me that it could be an actual place in the earth. I thought the skirt suit had to do with a change of ministerial office. The Lord had spoken to me in 2011, warning that change and transition was coming. I thought the garment represented a new mantle. Perhaps, so it did?

Back to October 2018, we were left standing near the south tower of Westminster. Once the age-old masonry was illuminated by the sun, I was released to move again. We found our way to the wooden door at the base of the tower. I had walked through that door in the vision. Though now, standing in that place, a barricade prevented further exploration. No matter, I knew what was on the other side of it.

Standing there in a bit of shock, I received understanding from the Lord that I would return there again someday to speak whatever the Lord wanted to say. He would see to it.

Turns out, the massive wooden doors of the south tower are known as the Queen's Entrance. It is the door through which the monarch passes when she enters to prepare for opening ceremonies. She is the only one ever allowed to pass through it. By law, it is the reigning monarch that opens the Houses of Parliament each year. It is the responsibility of the *Crown.*

From London we had scheduled a short side-trip to Northern Ireland. We took a quick flight over for a few days with friends. While in Belfast, we experienced there a rare hurricane. It swept across the whole of Ireland from the south to the north. She blustered her way across the island, dislodging anything not battened down. Her name was *Ophelia.*

Of all things: a hurricane named Ophelia, a vision about the Queen's door and tower; and the responsibility of the crown... What was God doing? He was revealing an assignment – a special operation He called Ophelia Crown. He had a job for us to do and we were on track to accomplish the task. We were walking a divine path of His planning and He had seen to it that we had all the confirmation we needed to proceed.

As an added note: a certain apostle said to me once, *"Deborah, you are like a hurricane. All a nation can do is brace for impact."*

None of us had any idea the magnitude of the full story until it was over.

God Will Have His Way

We returned to London with a team the following July (2019) with an invitation to tour the Houses of Parliament (Westminster). How we came by this invitation is not to be shared, in that tours of the Palace are not usually open to foreigners. Albeit no rules were broken, we will keep our sources close to the vest.

The Lord saw to it. He made a way where there was seemingly no way. Moreover, we were intent on walking through the door that only He could have opened for us. We were on assignment. *Operation Ophelia Crown* was about to commence.

Shortly before we took the team into the Palace of Westminster, the Lord gave us the words to speak. We walked the Queens' path starting near her entrance, through the robing room and onto the floor of the House of Lords. The tour then proceeded on to the House of Commons, as each team member declared repeatedly under our breath the Word of the Lord:

*God will have His way.
He will have His say
In this hour on this day!*

The Queen is never permitted to approach the House of Commons. It is against British law. Yet, our team walked right in, as if we knew what we were doing. Perhaps that makes us common?

The House of Commons is a large hall with many seats to accommodate all the Ministers of Parliament (MPs). On each side of the auditorium, there is a room. These rooms are used for a specific purpose. When there is a vote on the floor for consideration, an MP enters to the left and "yay" (yes) is marked next to his or her name on the attendance roster; an entry to the right is registered as a "nay" (no).

Turns out, on the day of our tour, there was a vote to be considered on the floor. Later that day, the House of Commons would reassemble to vote on a BREXIT deal put together between the Prime Minister and the European Union – supposedly the final agreement – not.

After the fact, we learned that dark forces had been trying to push through a bad deal before anyone really had time to read it. It could have crippled Britain's efforts to exit the EU in a timely manner.

When we entered the House of Commons that day, we were escorted by the tour guide through the "nay" side. Amazingly enough, when the tourists cleared and the members reassembled to vote, the majority of the MPs followed the same path, entering through the "nay" side of the chamber – including a significant delegation from Northern Ireland. It caused the plans of an unseen enemy to fail yet again.

The President of the United States made his first trip to London two days later. He arrived calling for the dismissal or resignation of the Prime Minister, supporting the man who would eventually replace her. Her successor went on to effectively lead Britain out of the European Union by God's design.

As in every other case, many were praying. Yet, God sent us half-way around the world in a *boots-on-the-ground* operation to be His voice at a time when He needed the powers of darkness to yield. We said what needed to be said to accomplish His purposes on His time clock.

The Sniper: A Unique Glimpse at a Special Operation of Prayer

In the grand scheme of things, our portion was a tiny spec in an ocean of petitions. We all have a role to play. This account is the only one we know to tell. Eternity will reveal a much bigger, broader perspective of what I suspect to be a massive covert operation under the direction of the Lord of Hosts.

The prayer endeavor w/ "prevail" "on our watch" Set to God's Time Clock

9/4/23

THE BIGGER THREAT

The following events actually happened with the dates being intermingled with other deployments. This particular account is about such a top-secret mission, there will be no documented articles provided. Take it for what it is worth. Yet, it happened just as it is detailed below.

A Three-Hour Trance

12 April 2018 turned out to be an eventful day. Between the hours of 6:30 a.m. and 9:30 a.m., I experienced what could only be termed a supernatural vision or trance. There was a lot to it, with many prophetic indicators:

> My husband and I were in an Asian country. It seemed to be an island, possibly in the south Pacific. We were gathered there with a group of ministers planning for a large evangelistic outreach.
>
> There was a secret society plotting something behind our backs. They were seemingly legitimate on the surface, but in secret they planned and schemed.

> *Privately, a friend whispered to me, "Something is not right here. Don't trust these people."*
>
> *They could not be trusted. Though they had elected to include us in their social gatherings and informal meetings, something was amiss. Secretly, I caught a glimpse of what appeared to be an ephod that they were trying to keep hidden. They used it in their private strategy sessions.*

In Bible times, the ephod was used to draw the borders and boundaries of Israel. Perhaps their evil plotting involved redrawing ancient boundaries?

As the vision progressed:

> *Suddenly news reached our ears that a nuclear facility was bombed on the north shore of the small island. It was reported that a neighboring superpower was the suspected bomber.*
>
> *We now found ourselves in a dire situation. What were we to do? We were in harm's way.*
>
> *Suddenly, a powerful woman of prayer (a woman of blessed memory) came to me. This was unusual, as she had been in eternity for*

many years. She poked her finger in my face and demanded, "Come with me!"

She took me to the site of the bombing and directed me on what to do. It was like we were working behind the veil - working together to minimize the radiation exuding from the damaged facility. She was with me every step of the way.

When we were finished with that work, she disappeared and I returned to my body in the hotel where we had been staying in the south. It brought great comfort to find there my spiritual mother and mentor helping to determine what to do next. Under the cover of night we escaped the city.

The next thing I knew, we were on U.S. soil watching wave after wave of war planes flying overhead. I had a sense they were American planes and that they were going off to war – World War III.

When I came to myself I was shaken. I knew it needed prayer right away and contacted one of my praying friends. As a mentor, she responded by saying, *"How do you recommend we proceed with this?"*

Note 1: The best teachers always know the right questions to ask.

We then developed a prayer strategy:

- Prayer for leadership was a key
- Praying for those things that are hidden to be revealed
- Taking our seat or standing in the place of authority.
- Prayer in the Spirit would bring additional clarity and direction.

Pray in the plans of God.

Note 2: Getting into the flow of the Spirit is the best thing we to do when we do not know what to do.

We had a sense that there was a real threat of something nuclear in Asia, but perhaps not in the way we had once thought. Much prayer had already been made regarding North Korea and their threats. Yet, we now had caught a glimpse of a much bigger threat looming to the south.

Our job as people of prayer is to pray in the plans of God and stop the strategies of the enemy. Not only did God reveal the strategies of darkness, but also the tool that was being used (the ephod) to develop it – whether symbolic or actual (Daniel 2:22). God establishes the borders of nations

(Acts 17:26). The key was contending for the boundaries God has set.

War in the Middle East is one thing; World War III is another thing entirely. Somewhere in the processing of the assignment, the Lord began talking to me about the war prophesied in Ezekiel 38. That war is actually *written*; it will surely come to pass. In my opinion, World War III would merely be a distraction devised by the enemy to take away from what God wants to reveal to the nations.

> ***Ezekiel 38:16*** *– ...that the nations may know Me* [God].

At some point I was also reminded of something the Lord said to me in October of 2016: *"Have I ever shown you anything that couldn't be changed by prayer."*

Many of our long term prayer assignments have brought us to such a time as this. With this deployment, the goal was (and still is) to be one of many who stand in the way of world war; to thwart the strategies of the enemy.

> ***Ephesians 1:22-23*** *- And hath put all things under his feet, and gave him to be the head over all things to the church, which is his body...*

The Church of the Lord Jesus Christ must awaken. We must understand our place of authority and our responsibility to use it. We are to reign over the powers of darkness. We are seated in a position of victory in Him.

Over the course of the months that followed, we were able to eventually identify the exact location of the nuclear facility and the island in question. Moreover, the threat loomed in our hearts day after day.

In August of that same year, my prayer mentor asked how things were going with the assignment. I replied that we sensed a need to perhaps put our feet on the ground there. She said she thought that sounded like a good idea.

The problem: we did not know a single soul in that portion of the world. We had no contacts – zero. We attempted several times to find someone, to no avail. Eventually we made a cold contact through a missions' organization. Their network subsequently put us in contact with a man who was willing to help us.

Flights were booked. We landed in an undisclosed location later that year. Oh, what a glorious day! And what an opportunity we stepped into!

Acts 17:26 *– And He has made from one blood every nation of men to dwell on all the face of the earth, and has determined their pre-appointed times and the boundaries of their dwellings,*

Daniel 2:22 *– He reveals deep and secret things; He knows what is in the darkness, And light dwells with Him.*

The Donkey

For the sake of time and space I will spare many of the details of the trip. We found great favor there. The Lord opened amazing doors that only He could have touched. We covered an immense amount of real estate in the 15 days of our excursion.

Amazingly enough we were able to find both locations from the vision. We stayed in the same hotel and toured the nuclear facility that had been seen in the Spirit so many months before. I will say the nuclear facility was in remarkably good condition compared to the state in which I had previously viewed it.

All along the way as we journeyed and with every new friend we met, eventually the conversation would lead to one man. Each person would say:

"Have you met the Donkey? You need to meet the Donkey." Apparently, I am not the only one with a God-breathed code name.

For the sake of anonymity, we will only refer to the man of God as the Donkey. He is an apostolic missionary of Middle Eastern descent. He was sent on assignment to the island. The Lord had decreed to him, *"You are 'Donkey,' for I will ride you over this entire island. You shall indeed carry the gospel to this people."*

He is a true apostle. His ministry brought a dramatic impact to these people and their land. For me, he was the only man on the island that could have validated the vision and the events seen on 12 April 2018.

We met for coffee in the capitol city for the first time, just before his team was to depart. As we exited the coffee shop, the Lord said, *"Tell him about the vision."* Walking down the street, I related the details to the Donkey. A look of shock and awe spread over his face. He asked, *"What was that date?!? I must go and check my journal."*

He then recounted being a personal witness to a military escalation on the island during a previous trip. He himself saw multiple planes in

The Bigger Threat

the air ready for battle. At the time, it was quite disturbing to him and his team.

He eventually made inquiry with a few military contacts. They were indeed able to confirm that war had been deterred. It was also confirmed that the confrontation was over an attempted border manipulation.

For the sake of security, we are not at liberty to share further details. It was and still is classified.

Upon his return to his home and his journal, the Donkey was able to verify the dates of the escalation being directly connected to the time of the vision and our subsequent prayers. Only God could have orchestrated such a divine operation.

THE SHOT HEARD 'ROUND THE WORLD

In the year 2019, along with a few international excursions, the Lord asked us to host a series of prayer seminars. Each one was unique with anointed guest speakers. Yet, all pale in comparison to the one held at the end of the year.

It seemed such an odd time to have a seminar what with the holidays and year-end vacations. 29-31 December were the dates the Lord insisted we set aside (Sunday night through Tuesday morning). My prayer mentor journeyed from another state and we were all set to gather in His name.

As the conference dates approached, I became slightly nervous in that I had no specific direction for the sessions. After hosting several conferences, I had become accustomed to presenting a theme on the first night. Yet, this time the only leading I had from the Holy Spirit had to do with a sermon on the subject of grace. I dismissed it entirely, thinking it did not fit with a *prayer* conference.

Upon the teacher's arrival, she assured me not to worry. She had received direction from the Lord. She would cast vision during her first session. On the morning 30 December, she opened the Book to Ezekiel chapter 38 and masterfully made the case for praying about war.

I will be frank in saying that I was not necessarily comfortable with this idea – especially to pray about the war involving Israel. Ezekiel 38 hits a little too close to the last of the last days for me. Yes, it is written. Yes, it shall surely come to pass. Yet, my mind would argue, *"Is it really necessary for me to get involved? Surely someone else is better suited to lead this type of prayer."*

The teacher firmly caught my attention with one simple truth – the truth from verse 16, *"...that the nations may know"* Him. With a heart for the lost and a passion for the great end-time harvest, I could see how God could use such a war as a witness to fuel a worldwide ingathering of souls.

As she wrapped up the session, she said, *"I don't even know how to pray about war."* And in the very next moment, I heard the Holy Spirit say in my heart, *"You know what to do."*

I had already received all the direction I needed. The pieces finally came together. The sermon on grace was the missing link. Why the grace of God? Because really, the only way Israel could ever win such a war – a war against all odds – would truly be by the grace of God.

We came into the conference that night ready to pray. The Lord helped me lay it out very carefully as to the need and value of grace in such situations.

There is no way to convey on the printed page the power of the corporate anointing we stepped into that night. The entire congregation eagerly and swiftly moved into the heavenly realms to take a position. They were there for one reason: to release the grace of God on behalf of the nation of Israel.

We went up into the heavenly realms and then moved eastward toward Israel. It was smooth and easy, no struggle, no fight. We were working from a position only found in Christ – the one where He is seated far above (Ephesians 1:21, 3:10, Colossians 1:16, Ephesians 6:12). We shouted grace to the mountain and made tremendous power available (Zechariah 4:7, James 5:16).

As we wrapped up the session, an apostle seated in the back of the auditorium moved to the podium. (This is the same man who had previously referred to me as a hurricane.) He was clearly moved by the Holy Spirit.

He started by saying something like, *"Strange things always happen when I get around this woman."* He mentioned some personal things the Lord had shown him regarding his own ministry. He then went on to recount something that still burns in my heart to this day. He said:

> *As we were praying, the Lord asked me a question. He said, "What happened on April 19, 1775?"*
>
> *I did not know. The Lord said, "Look it up."*
>
> *When I looked it up I found it was the first day of the Revolutionary War. It was the occurrence commonly known as the day "the shot heard 'round the world" was fired.*

Continuing, he shared that he believed that what we had just witnessed in this prayer meeting was like unto that event. That:

> *...there would be something that would mark this meeting as 'a shot fired that would be heard around the world.'*

The Shot Heard 'Round the World

It was a moment similar to 11 December 2003. Remember the chapter: *Treasure in a Hole?* Our little prayer group left not knowing the magnitude of what was done? And then three days later we learned about the capture of Saddam Hussein? This meeting closed with that same sort of unspoken, sober expectancy.

The date was 30 December 2019. What had we done? We did not know. <u>We were not going to touch it with our thought lives.</u> We had followed the leading of the Spirit and we were going to leave it in His hands for another day – whatever that day may be.

For the sake of record, we should point out the nations of prophecy involved in the Ezekiel 38 war are, of course, Israel, along with Iran, Turkey, and perhaps Russia. According to scripture, it is a battle Israel is foretold to win quite supernaturally.

Three days after we prayed on 30 December, a despotic Iranian terrorist was reported as being killed in a drone strike. At the time, he was considered the world's most notorious and dangerous terrorist.

Many petitions over many years had been made before the Father regarding this man's capture or demise. The end of his reign of terror actually occurred on 3 January 2020 in that part of the world; 2 January from where we stood, considering the time difference, approximately three days from when we had prayed.[20]

On 3 January 2020, one of my favorite end-time Bible teachers released a blog answering this question: *"Do today's events have to do with Ezekiel 38 war?* Her answer: *"Probably. They are at least a preamble to the war of Ezekiel 38. How long the 'preamble' lasts is unknown to us."*[21]

For the many weeks that followed, Bible teachers, ministers and commentators alike spoke of *the shot heard 'round the world.* Not one of them knew the details of our story or the implications thereof. I am certain ours is only one of many.

> **Ephesians 1:21** – *far above all principality and power and might and dominion, and every name that is named, not only in this age but also in that which is to come.*
>
> **Ephesians 3:10** – *to the intent that now the manifold wisdom of God might be made known by the church to the principalities and powers in the heavenly places*
>
> **Colossians 1:16** – *For by Him all things were created that are in heaven and that are on*

earth, visible and invisible, whether thrones or dominions or principalities or powers. All things were created through Him and for Him.

Zechariah 4:7 - *Who [are] you, O great mountain?... you shall become a plain! And he shall bring forth the capstone with shouts of "Grace, grace to it!"*

James 5:16 - *...The effective, fervent prayer of a righteous man avails much.*

SETTING THINGS IN ORDER

Warning: the reader may need his or her steel-toed combat boots for this chapter.

Submission & Accountability

Basically, there are two kinds of snipers: soldiers and criminals. There is a distinct line that separates the two.

A sniper should be one who is held accountable; one who willingly places himself under authority. He takes orders from one greater than himself, from someone who sees a bigger picture than what can be viewed through the snipers scope. He has no plans of his own. He follows orders.

Criminals are accountable only to themselves and willingly yield to lawlessness. Very often, snipers gone rogue are the ones who work alone.

In case the reader has not already surmised, this author has no background in the military. Yet, it should be said that we are firmly *under authority*. We (the over-watch and I) willingly submit to a power greater than ourselves. Moreover, that submission is not just to God alone. There are others in our lives to wh[om we are] accountable.

We are blessed to have a [pastor who serves not] only as a shepherd of the [flock but also in the] office of the apostle. We ar[e blessed that he keeps us] informed of what the Lo[rd has placed upon his] hearts. He knows who we ar[e and what we do. We] sometimes travel to the nat[ions with him as part] of a team. He has been known to attend our conferences and opens his pulpit to us from time to time.

There are other men and women of God that we have collected over the years – mentors and friends. This book will have been in their hands long before it ever goes to press.

Publishing a work like this is something we do not take lightly. For the purposes of instruction and example, we are putting things out that would normally be kept hidden in our hearts. Do not think for a moment that we have not vetted this work thoroughly before its release. It has been bathed in prayer and covered entirely under the blood of Christ.

Moreover we submit ourselves to the word of God. It is our supreme authority in life. We endeavor to operate with a full understanding of

Setting Things in Order

what is written and follow the guidelines presented therein. If something does not line up with the Bible, then we will likely set it on the shelf until the Lord sheds further light on it. Time and space has prevented us from building deep doctrinal foundations in this book, but rest assured that we have taken time to develop a firm grasp of the Word in our own personal lives.

> People of prayer must be those who are willing to submit to authority. If one wishes to walk in authority, he or she must first learn to yield to authority. One who is not accountable can be dangerous or destructive to the kingdom of God. If not dangerous, in the least they would be found unproductive, ineffective or unfruitful. The Lord cannot trust those who will not listen to Him or want to follow their own way.

[handwritten annotations: "until 8/16/23 – Roxie", "God changed me", "up"]

We want to reiterate that snipers very seldom work alone. Special operations teams usually have several members. The sniper is a team player and one who must be willing to work with others. In the military, special operations teams are extremely close and move as one unit. Every sniper must understand the importance and operation of unity (Ephesians 4:1-3).

[handwritten: 1 Cor 1:10]

The sniper does not arbitrarily pick his target. He is deployed on missions. He is not the judge and jury. He is the agent of change. He is humble, knowing that he is only one member of many and that he only sees in part. He is responsible to do what is set before him – no more, no less.

> At the end of the day, all the glory goes to God. It is only by the hand of God that a sniper succeeds. It is only by the blood of Christ that he is covered and protected. It is only by the mercy of God that he returns safely into the loving arms of his family and friends.

Ephesians 4:1-3 – [1]*I, therefore, the prisoner of the Lord, beseech you to walk worthy of the calling with which you were called,* [2]*with all lowliness and gentleness, with longsuffering, bearing with one another in love,* [3]*endeavoring to keep the unity of the Spirit in the bond of peace.*

Satisfying
Noticing
Intentional
Present
ER

Submitting
Nurturing
Intentional
Prayer
Eternally
Relevant

SNIPER

THE TESTIMONY OF WITNESSES

Imagine for a moment what the men who journeyed with the Apostle Paul would have shared given an opportunity. Listed below are actual accounts from men and women of God who are witnesses to some of the events described in this book.

The Prophet

There are certain occurrences that take place in one's life that one never forgets. They become implanted in our memory as something that changed us such as the birth of a child, the assassination of a president, or a nation-shaking terrorist attack. We remember the exact moment where we were and what we were doing.

In the spiritual realm, there are events that mark us in like manner, moments in time we will never forget. Such events might be the day we receive Christ as Lord and Savior or the first time we lead someone to Christ.

The first time I preached a sermon on a street corner was at the age of ten. In response, a man staggered out of a bar across the street. He became completely sober as he knelt at my feet to recite the sinner's prayer and accept Christ as his Lord and Savior.

Like it was yesterday, I remember well the first time I ever spoke the Word of the Lord to someone about God's plan for his life. Not to mention the day God called me His prophet. These are instances that live in my mind and heart forever!

Many are the memories I have of Northern Ireland: the powerful meetings, the people we met, and the sights we saw. Yet all these pale in the light of what took place at Stormont. All that is written in this book is an accurate and true account of what took place that day when we as a group visited the building. Yet, as a prophet I feel there is much more to say.

That morning as we prepared to visit this historical site, there was a stirring in my spirit. Even though we did not speak it out loud, we all knew that we were on a divine appointment. In our hearts, we knew this was more than a tour. It was part of God's ordained agenda that would impact the lives of many and the future of Ireland. It was to be a God encounter. The door had opened so quickly for us we knew God must have had a purpose in mind.

As we toured Stormont we were given full access to both assembly halls. While in each chamber we prayed over every seat. The presence of God seemed to increase as we went deeper into the heart of the building.

The last room we entered was on the uppermost floor, the strategy room of the leading political party. As we entered, the presence of God's glory was already there waiting for us. Unlike the author of this book, I did not see any angels, but I knew they were there because I felt their presence just as I had many times before.

As a prophet of God, I was expecting the Lord to give me a prophetical word for this occasion. However, that was not in God's plan. Instead, we entered into a time prayer. Hands were placed upon our host and different members of the group prayed prophetical prayers.

I remember as I prayed, the one thing the Holy Spirit emphasized was for me to request a spirit of revelation be imparted upon the nation. As God's prophet I was instructed to make a petition. The Lord required a heartfelt plea, one that revealed my love for the nation and people. It seemed everyone who prayed, made pleas that would move the heart of God.

After the last prayer was said, we all stood in silence, knowing that what had just taken place would somehow shake the nation. Little did we know what would transpire in the weeks that followed?

As we left the room, to myself I thought it strange that this strategy room was on the uppermost floor of the building. All at once I was shaken by the Holy Spirit as He spoke to me and said:

> "The room you just left will become known as The Upper Room of Ireland. It is here in this room where both political parties will unite as one in prayer to break strongholds and bring revival to the land!"

Signed,
His Prophet

The Apostle

Reading this book takes me back to the very day we entered into the Stormont complex in Belfast, Northern Ireland. The large building where government sits is imposing. As well as the many life changing decisions made there, it has also been the staging point for a myriad of other events including protests and prayer vigils.

I was there as part of an apostolic team made up of local and international leaders including the author of this book. Our assignment was to pray over the nation in the very place from which it is governed. Our hosts were the leading political group and party of our First Minister. After some hospitality and discussion our hosts were keen to get down to prayer.

Various prayers were released from many perspectives. A common theme could be heard: righteousness exalting a nation (Proverbs 14:34). I was personally touched to hear our international friends praying with such earnest passion on behalf of my country. Any unrighteousness was called out and required to be exposed. The voices united with resounding words of affirmation.

Within days the government had fallen into what became a long period of shut down. This was largely due to the disclosure of questionable decisions made by some regarding funding in a particular arena. The country fell into chaos. Front page news for many months, the press was all over it.

It took around three years for the power sharing executive to come back together after what was a watershed period. I have no doubt having been in attendance and privy to what took place in that Stormont prayer meeting, it impacted our government significantly. It brought forth sanctification, and a fresh impetus – some reasons only eternity may reveal.

This assignment was yet another occasion for me to get to know the author of this book. I understand her to be a seasoned minister with many years of experience in different fields within God's kingdom. She is a "safe pair of hands" who can be relied upon when needed. I have enjoyed the company of her and her husband in conversations often. She is feisty, focused and uncompromising – right up my street.

On one occasion we were ministering at the altar as part of a national apostolic event. As we moved through the crowd, God led me to pray for this woman (the author of this book). As I began, a word dropped into my spirit. God revealed to me that she was His (My) "Battle Ax."

Can you imagine my thought: Having to tell a feisty, focused, uncompromising woman of God that she is a "Battle Ax?" Of course, I knew immediately that this was a complimentary word from God to her. As it were, He sees her as an effective prayer warrior and minister.

The years of faithful and dedicated prayer have led to the release of this material. I know there have been other books but the timing of this book is impeccable. This author, led by the Lord, has emphasized the absolute necessity of increased, effective prayer in these days.

Not only must prayer increase, but also the nature of it must change. Only this will accommodate what the Lord wants to achieve through the church in the close of the age.

Wineskins are being renewed and changed. Paradigms are being shifted. Church cultures are being challenged. Prayer is the ignition for it all.

We must move into a place where our prayers once again shake things loose. Aggressive, unrelenting, uncompromising prayer must be the order of our time. We must invite the Lord of hosts, Jehovah Saboath into the battle with us. We must invoke His strong right arm on our behalf.

An activation of heavens armies is required with the reopening of kingdom portals. Such efforts will enable the angelic host to come back and forth, ministering with the church on behalf of our great Commander in Chief.

The blood and the name of Jesus is our cry as we move forward appropriating the promises of God by faith as we go. It is essential for some to find a new passion. For others, there is a need to rediscover the fire they have lost.

Our greatest challenge is that of distraction. It seems everything grabs our attention. We

The Testimony of Witnesses

live in days where the apostle Paul told us that men would be lovers of pleasure more than lovers of God (2 Timothy 3:1-5). Social media, entertainment, leisure, politics and dare I say it, even ministry have become our nemesis.

I once wrote in an article, "The level of devotion to anything can be measured by the amount of time invested in it." We must resist the temptation to be distracted and ask for God's grace in helping to redeem the time.

This book is an antidote to the spirit of the age. It is an encouragement and a provocation. WE MUST PRAY!!!!! There is no room for debate or disagreement on this absolute truth.

To pursue means to run after with hostile intent. To truly pursue God, the culture of one's life must adapt to the level of pursuit.

We must make time for prayer. It must become our priority as opposed to something we do when we have time. The nations are at stake. Eternal results are hanging in the balance.

"I beseech thee therefore brethren by the mercies of God..." that you "...pray without ceasing" (Romans 12:1a; 1 Thessalonians 5:17 - KJV).

Signed,
The Apostle from Across the Pond

2 Timothy 3:1-5 – *[1]But know this, that in the last days perilous times will come: [2]For men will be lovers of themselves, lovers of money, boasters, proud, blasphemers, disobedient to parents, unthankful, unholy, [3]unloving, unforgiving, slanderers, without self-control, brutal, despisers of good, [4]traitors, headstrong, haughty, lovers of pleasure rather than lovers of God, [5]having a form of godliness but denying its power. And from such people turn away!*

Romans 12:1 – *I beseech you therefore, brethren, by the mercies of God, that you present your bodies a living sacrifice, holy, acceptable to God, which is your reasonable service.*

1 Thessalonians 5:17 – *pray without ceasing*

The Teacher

In the reading of these rich and engaging adventures in the Holy Spirit, I kept hearing the words of **John 16:13-15**:

> [13] *However, when He, the Spirit of truth, has come, He will guide you into all truth; for He will not speak on His own authority, but whatever He hears He will speak; and He will tell you things to come.* [14] *He will glorify Me, for He will take of what is Mine and declare it to you.* [15] *All things that the Father has are Mine. Therefore I said that He will take of Mine and declare it to you.*

This book gives voice to some of the secrets of prayer that the adversary has been so want to silence over the centuries. And I must echo the author: It seems that now is the time for those of us who have seen and heard to begin sharing some of our secrets for the sake of the next generation.

It is my opinion that, in these last days, the Body of Christ is learning to access these secrets of prayer (Ephesians 6:18) more efficiently and accurately than ever before. We may not all be 'snipers,' but we can all *become 'sharp shooters' in the Spirit. These fascinating accounts will change, equip, and inspire you on your path.*

For the sake of record, I was there the night "the shot fired heard 'round the world" rang out. It happened just as it has been detailed in a previous chapter. I am a witness.

Signed,
The Instigator

Ephesians 6:18 – *praying always with all prayer and supplication in the Spirit, being watchful to this end with all perseverance and supplication for all the saints—*

The Donkey

This book is a gift to the charismatic and Spirit-filled community – full and richly textured in these vital elements of Spirit-led Christianity for today's church.

There are many challenges to the truth in the world today: false doctrines, twisted teachings, parallel truths, subjective positions, diluted convictions and quicksand principles. These challenges skew interpretation, all for the sake of tickling the ear and presenting a comfortable gospel. We must return to the time of absolutes – where God's Word is the overall authority on matters concerning each aspect of our lives and existence.

This is a time in our history where the Church is moving to another level of uncovering mysteries and the hidden wisdom of God (1 Corinthians 2:7). Praise God for His anointed servant, the sniper and author of this book. She has through prayer, dedication and commitment stayed in His presence long enough to know what God is saying to the Church in these days.

This book gives insightful teaching and a prophetic gift throughout the pages set before you.

I recall the things written of me in this blessed text. As a witness, I happily confirm the truth of the narrative.

Shalom In Jesus Name,
The Donkey

1 Corinthians 2:7 – *But we speak the wisdom of God in a mystery, the hidden wisdom which God ordained before the ages for our glory,*

The Apostolic Pastor

Looking through the glasses of one who is very blessed and humbled to do God's Kingdom work on His earth, I am always at odds and many times struggle with taking any sort of a title. I find it difficult to claim any sort of position other than that of a servant.

I am totally blessed, honored in fact, that the Lord has allowed me to witness first-hand some of the events written and recorded in this book. They were God moments, special seasons, divine timing, and ordained gatherings. I encourage the reader to pay very special attention, for the Lord intends to move each of us into an awareness of God's divine plan in which participation is an open door.

Many individuals described in this book are a driving force of encouragement to me as a minister. Constantly, they help to set me in forward motion. They continue to be a fresh breath to my calling and an endorphin to the very blood in my spiritual veins.

The author of this book and her over-watch (her husband and life-long partner) are included in the above statements. Their knowledge, experience and calling often bring completion to the loose ends that God wants to bring together. Simply, they serve much like the proverbial paint brush, flowing with the Holy Spirit to bring clarity, focus and direction to things seen, but more often to things not.

I remember vividly Northern Ireland. With great fear and trepidation I had received the assignment to prepare a team to minister in a city in the north. Along with many others, there were several five-fold ministers gathering those who would minister the gospel of Christ in all of Ireland.

In preparation, advance groups were traveling in and out of Ireland to spy out the land, to assemble and to pray. I was blessed to be numbered among those mentioned in this book, the apostolic team that visited the Stormont complex in Belfast, Northern Ireland.

This very grand building, the seat of government (that can be compared to the U.S. Capitol) was one of the places we found ourselves stepping into. Later on, many of these same team members would find themselves sitting with and praying in the chambers of local government in the city of Belfast. We were then honored to have opportunity to lay hands on and pray with the Mayor of the city.

At various times, on many other occasions, several of the ministers spoken of in this book have been found in other nations (including our own). It is awesome to be able to pray over regions from the very places of government. We have been firsthand witnesses of the supernatural movement that takes place when an apostolic team (made up of local and international leaders) follows the direction set forth by the Holy Spirit for a specific assignment. Cities, states, regions, and even nations shift and move, shaking at the sweep of God's mighty hand.

I can, as an eyewitness, agree with the accounts of the day at Stormont and the supernatural pieces that fell into place because somebody prayed!

As I have read the words contained in this book, I am reminded of something the Lord spoke in the third chapter of First Samuel. It provides a warning to the body of Christ to be heeded even now. Verse one:

> *"...The word of the Lord was rare and precious in those days; there was no frequent or widely spread vision"*

I encourage you to finish reading this book and share it with many others, for the nations are needy. The only healing that can take place will come through prayer and the word of God being released. God's presence must be allowed to be set in place, establishing once again wide spread vision to set forth God's plan in the earth.

Signed,
The Apostolic Pastoral SERVANT

The Other Apostle

I am the one who declared "the shot heard 'round the world." It happened just as described.

In this prayer conference I had not been at the day sessions, so I was not necessarily in tune with the flow that was taking place. When we started going up, at first for me it was awkward. I was new to this way of praying.

However, I was not new to hearing the voice of the Lord. When the Lord spoke "the shot heard around the world" I immediately sat down and started to look up the details. I then began to ask the Lord, "Why did you say this to me?"

About three minutes later I hear these words being spoken from the direction of pulpit: "Apostle, do you have anything?"

This book, "The Sniper," is more than a collection of testimonies and stories in regards to prayer. It brings to light an effective way of praying into God's appointed targets.

*Signed,
The Other Apostle*

The Other Sniper

First of all, I would like to thank the author of this book for allowing me to read over this manuscript. It presents powerful examples that demonstrate God's strategic plans for the nations of the world.

This book will encourage and inspire the body of Christ to dive deeper into prayer. It

The Testimony of Witnesses

will excite and encourage, equip and open the eyes of the Church to the power and importance of taking our place in Him. Everyone in the body of Christ can contribute a supernatural and significant supply to the plans of God globally.

"The Sniper" gives us a real life look of how God uses specific and precise prayer moments to accomplish His strategic operations around the world. Standing in Christ's authority, covered by the Blood and yielded to the Holy Spirit's leading in prayer will have profound impact upon the nations. Our country, states, cities, communities, our block + even our home *I had the privilege to travel with the prayer team to Ireland in the spring of 2017. We all felt it was a God-given, special assignment as we traveled the island. There were several significant breakthroughs as we journeyed, visiting many brethren and historical sights.*

One of those breakthroughs came when we visited the Peace Bridge located in Derry/Londonderry, Northern Ireland. It took place just as it has been described. God set us up at that precise place and time to take the sniper shot in prayer. It was just what was needed to reveal the deception and boasting of a troubled nation. God's timing and positioning for our team was once again perfect.

I believe this book is so important to the body of Christ because it reveals that every person and every branch in God's army makes a significant supply. It is a truth; sometimes snipers are needed to take that precise shot in prayer.

My life has been hugely impacted by the ministry of and friendship with this author and her husband. They have taught me to pray at a level that I never experienced before. Our times together are by far some of my favorite moments in the Lord's service. They have believed in me as a person of prayer and encouraged me to go further in Christ.

Signed,
The Other Sniper

The Other Over-Watch

I was there the day the admonition to "look in that hole" was released. I heard the plea to "see that treasure in that hole." We all stood in awe at the presence of God, wondering *what it the world had just happened. I remember well the moment we discovered the end result of what had been prayed that day. There are no words to describe the lumps that formed in our throats as we understood how God had used us.*

Yes, I was there when prayer was made regarding North Korea; there, pushing the sniper into position. I was there when we detected their tactics were nothing more than lies and rhetoric. From the anointing upon us, it was easy to know that the powers of darkness had taken notice of the ultimatum placed upon them... Mute!

Standing over-watch at the base of the Peace Bridge in Derry/Londonderry, I had been the one who discovered the news article about the escalation. It happened just as has been described.

I was also was there the day Operation Ophelia Crown launched in the Palace of Westminster. I was only one member on team, but it was thrilling to be able to declare that God would have His way; He would have His say.

I was there in the auditorium when we prayed in unity, shouting "grace" toward Israel and the war of Ezekiel 38. I remember well, three days later learning what it meant to fire "the shot heard 'round the world."

As a matter of fact, I've been there on most of this journey – humbled and honored, speechless at the awesome ways of God.

I believe this book is so important to the Body of Christ because it will become a critical manual for training in prayer; it will be especially important as the body of Christ walks out these things on the earth. We need to be fully equipped and trained just like the elite warriors we are. We each need to learn the role we have been called to fulfill and step into the missions God would have us to accomplish.

*Signed,
The Other Over-Watch*

Closing Thoughts

Why write a book in such a manner? Why not tell who we are and be more specific about our individual lives?

For too long, the Body of Christ has been distracted by the reputations of men. The individuals associated with this book are not interested in building their own names. They understand the importance of the message without needing to be known. What is important is that **He** is known, that God is glorified with His people being edified and equipped.

The Apostle Paul wrote an interesting dialogue is 2 Corinthians 12:

> ***2 Corinthians 12:2-6*** *– ²I know a man in Christ who fourteen years ago--whether in the body I do not know, or whether out of the body I do not know, God knows--such a one was caught up to the third heaven. ³And I know such a man--whether in the body or out of the body I do not know, God knows-- ⁴how he was caught up into Paradise and heard inexpressible words, which it is not lawful for a man to utter. ⁵Of such a one I will boast; yet of myself I will not boast, except in my infirmities. ⁶For though I might desire to boast, I will not be a fool; for I will speak the truth. But I refrain, lest anyone should think of me above what he sees me to be or hears from me.*

Most theologians will readily agree that the man of whom he speaks is likely no one other than the testifier himself. Whether Paul or someone else, it is clear the visionary saw a need to distance himself from such a profound revelation. Perhaps he was concerned about persecution. Perhaps he wanted to draw no attention to himself. Humility often requires an anonymous position.

For centuries, men and women of God have been privy to divine secrets and revelations, but challenged to share what they knew for the sake of humility. There is a need to glorify God and draw away from our own individual identity in the grand scheme. Yes, it is important to know who we are in Christ. Yet, apart from Him, we are nothing. We have come to a time when we must find a way for some divine secrets to be shared.

The Sniper is nothing close to what Paul described of the heavenly experience. Yet, there is a need to guard and protect that which is precious. God is revealing Himself in ways that must be understood in this the last of the last days.

> **Romans 12:3** – *For I say, through the grace given to me, to everyone who is among you,* **not to think of himself more highly than he ought to think***, but to think soberly, as God has dealt to each one a measure of faith.*

The Testimony of Witnesses

John 3:27, 29-30 – *²⁷John answered and said, "A man can receive nothing unless it has been given to him from heaven...²⁹He who has the bride is the bridegroom; but the friend of the bridegroom, who stands and hears him, rejoices greatly because of the bridegroom's voice. Therefore this joy of mine is fulfilled.* **³⁰He must increase, but I must decrease.**

Amen

There is a need to glorify God

9/6/23

RESOURCES

[1] "World War I" – https://en.wikipedia.org/wiki/World_War_I
[2] "Yugoslavia" – https://en.wikipedia.org/wiki/Yugoslavia#Succession,_2006%E2%80%93present
[3] "Czechoslovakia" – https://en.wikipedia.org/wiki/Czechoslovakia
[4] "Eastern Bloc" – https://en.wikipedia.org/wiki/Eastern_Bloc
[5] "Gorbachev Puts Off His Journey to Czechoslovakia" – https://www.nytimes.com/1987/04/06/world/gorbachev-puts-off-his-journey-to-czechoslovakia.html
[6] "Fall of the Berlin Wall" – https://en.wikipedia.org/wiki/Fall_of_the_Berlin_Wall
[7] "Dissolution of Czechoslovakia" – https://en.wikipedia.org/wiki/Dissolution_of_Czechoslovakia
[8] "Breakup of Yugoslavia" – https://en.wikipedia.org/wiki/Breakup_of_Yugoslavia
[9] "North Korea Famine" –

https://en.wikipedia.org/wiki/North_Korean_famine

[10] "Northern Ireland Riots" – https://en.wikipedia.org/wiki/1969_Northern_Ireland_riots

[11] "Peace Bridge" – https://en.wikipedia.org/wiki/Peace_Bridge_(Foyle)

[12] "War in Afghanistan" – https://en.wikipedia.org/wiki/War_in_Afghanistan_(2001%E2%80%93present)

[13] "2003 Invasion of Iraq" – https://en.wikipedia.org/wiki/2003_invasion_of_Iraq

[14] "Operation Red Dawn" – https://en.wikipedia.org/wiki/Operation_Red_Dawn

[15] "RHI Scandal: McGinness Calls on NI First Minister to Step Aside" – https://www.bbc.com/news/uk-31489031

[16] "NI Energy Scheme Failure 'Not Due to Corruption'" – https://www.bbc.com/news/uk-northern-ireland-38323577

[17] "Martin McGinness" – https://en.wikipedia.org/wiki/Martin_McGuinness

[18] "Northern Ireland: Devolution Formally Restored as Power-Sharing Resumes at Stormont" – https://news.sky.com/story/northern-ireland-devolution-formally-restored-as-power-sharing-resumes-at-stormont-11906096

[19] "UK's House of Commons Gives Final Approval for BREXIT Deal" – https://www.france24.com/en/20200109-uk-s-house-of-commons-gives-final-approval-for-brexit-deal

[20] "Assassination of Qasem Soleimani" – https://en.wikipedia.org/wiki/Assassination_of_Qasem_Soleimani

[21] "Ezekiel 38 War" – https://billyebrim.org/ezekiel-38-war/

ABOUT THE AUTHOR

It seems as though I have always been a bit of a warrior. From my youth, I would often be rebuked for having a razor-sharp tongue. Gentleness does not come naturally to me, though it is promised as a fruit of the Spirit (Galatians 5:22-23). As a pastor it plagued me. Far too often I would come across as harsh. I often complained to the Lord about it not wanting to injure the tender hearts of the sheep.

In March of 2011, the Lord promised that change would come:

> *Heart-warming and gentle you shall be. The impossible shall surely come to pass.*

It started in the spring of 2017 when three little honey bees mistook our front door for their hive. On the threshold, they left for us there three piles of golden pollen. We took it as a sign of good things to come as we left to lead a prayer team abroad. Everywhere we went in Ireland, honey bees would follow. We would pray; they would come.

Upon our return to the States, the Lord led me to a passage in the book of Judges about Samson. It was the story of the lion on the road and how Samson took honey from the carcass. He received this riddle:

> **Judges 14:14** – Out of the eater comes something to eat; **out of the strong comes something sweet.**

The following Sunday, our pastor released a message about Deborah from the book of Judges. He described the mantle she carried. He spoke of the important voice she had during her days of leadership in Israel. She spoke with a voice of: authority, clarity, submission, unity, and judgment – one who sat things in order according to the law of order.

The following spring and summer, the honey bees returned to our front door – only this time their queen decided to join them. We returned from a long trip down the Mississippi to find her in the middle of our living room floor.

A precious prophet and friend then said to me, "Don't you know! All of creation knows who you are." Deborah defined means Queen Bee.

By now, the reader should understand that "B." stands for "Battle-Ax" – which was also revealed during this same season in the course of 2017.

About the Author

The Lord has ways of teaching us who we are and what we are to do for Him.

In the fall of 2017 I had an encounter with one of the leading prophets of the land. Having great expectation as to what he might say, in his approach toward me he was found nearly speechless and stammering. After a long, rambling discourse about the massive heat generated by the old-fashioned pot-bellied stoves, he turned to me and said:

> *There's a fire in you! You know it. The Father knows it. Jesus knows it. The Holy Ghost knows it. And... the devil knows it and he wants nothing to do with you. You remind him of his destiny.*

In essence, the man called me a pot-bellied stove of which Vogelzang is a leading manufacturer.

Interesting enough, *zang* is also found in Mandarin Chinese. It means *storehouse* which is the story yet to be written. It will not be long now before we turn the page to the next assignment.

Deborah B. Vogelzang

Galatians 5:22-23 – ²²But the fruit of the Spirit is love, joy, peace, longsuffering, kindness, goodness, faithfulness, ²³gentleness, self-control. Against such there is no law.

could not see it, the wind was loud!

Oh, the Holy Spirit ——

9/4 this morning I sat outside & read again on the back pool where I could receive all of the peace, relaxation & quiet (other than the) needed to start such another wonderful day. As I put my head down into a ~~steadynes~~ steadied posture to see, look & read the words of the pages of the Bible the noise that exerted overwhelmed me — The loud sound of the branches rustling amongst themselves nor was it the hustle of the leaves moving on the branches, the noise I heard was the sound of a mighty RUSHING WIND! As I looked to notice that it was the wind was loud & I laughed marveled & laughed some more